How to be a Happy Cat

Charles Platt

Cartoons by Gray Jolliffe

LONDON
Victor Gollancz Ltd
1986

For Jodie and Scout

With thanks to Janet Morris,
Edward Bryant and Liz Knights

Design by Craig Dodd

First published in Great Britain 1986
by Victor Gollancz Ltd,
14 Henrietta Street, London WC2E 8QJ

A Gollancz Paperback

British Library Cataloguing in Publication Data
Platt, Charles
    How to be a happy cat.
    1. Cats — Humor
    I. Title   II. Jolliffe, Gray
    636.8'00207   SF445.5
ISBN 0-575-03991-4
ISBN 0-575-03902-7 Pbk

Photoset in Great Britain by
Rowland Phototypesetting Ltd,
Bury St Edmunds, Suffolk
Printed in Finland by Werner Söderström Oy

Contents

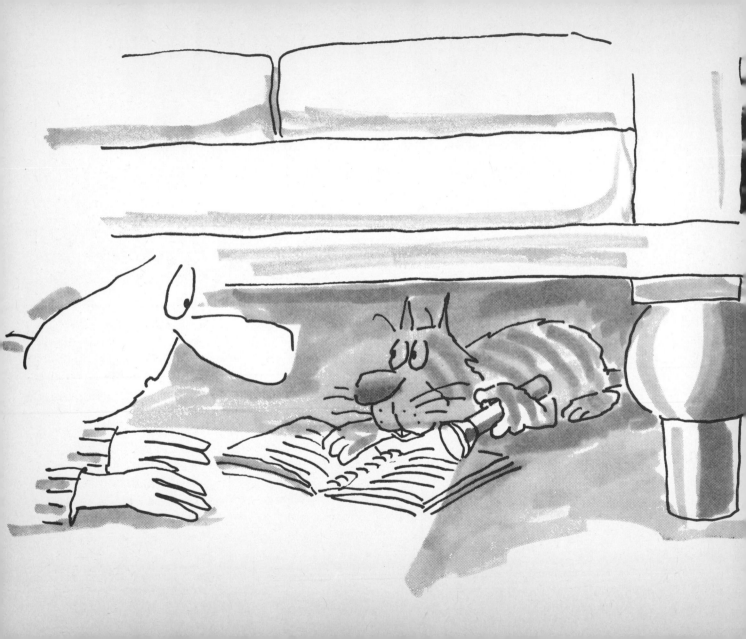

Foreword from the Translator

I woke suddenly in the middle of the night. There had been a noise that sounded like something falling. I lay and listened, but my small flat was silent, now, except for the distant murmur of traffic.

The clock beside my bed told me it was just past three. I decided to go back to sleep and forget the whole thing; but a couple of minutes later I realized I was still lying wide awake, wondering what it was I'd heard.

I slid out of bed, put on my dressing gown and stepped cautiously into the darkened living room. I paused in the doorway and blinked, unable to make sense of what I saw. The carpet was lit by a strange, faint yellow glow, which seemed to be coming from under the sofa. I crept forward, dropped down onto my hands and knees—and came nose to nose with George, my ginger cat.

We stared at each other, and it's hard to say which of us looked more surprised. He was crouched on the floor beside my torch, which he had filched from its usual place in one of the kitchen drawers. Somehow he had managed to drag it under the sofa and switch it on. Even more bizarre, its dim beam was directed at the pages of a battered Woolworth's notebook that he was holding open on the floor between his paws.

After a moment George crawled out from his hiding place and walked calmly into the kitchen, as if nothing was out of the ordinary and he thought he might get a midnight snack. I was not so easily fooled, however. I reached under the sofa for my torch, then retrieved the notebook. When I examined it, I found to my surprise that its pages were covered in crude little ballpoint drawings, like Egyptian hieroglyphics.

At first I suspected an elaborate hoax. Over the next few days, however, I came to the inescapable conclusion that the drawings were some kind of primitive pictorial language. After many hours of careful study, I finally managed to decode their meaning. Quite simply, the little notebook turned out to be a comprehensive, state-of-the-art, self-help manual written by a cat for fellow felines. *How to be a Happy Cat* is my translation of that book.

Some readers may find this hard to believe. The evidence, however, is overwhelming. Cats have always had a reputation for being devious. They act innocent, but are undoubtedly smarter than they let on. Moreover, in recent years they have had unprecedented opportunities to educate themselves. How many of us have noticed them watching *Blue Peter*, the *Nine O'Clock Mews* and other TV programmes with unnaturally close attention? As this book shows, cats aren't just looking at the pictures. They've been listening and learning, and biding their time.

At first, I couldn't work out how George had come into possession of the notebook. Then I remembered he had stayed overnight at the vet just a few days previously. A cat must have given it to him there, and he could have hidden it under the blanket in his basket. To judge from the condition of my torch batteries, George had been studying the notebook for two or three nights before I caught him. No doubt he planned eventually to pass it on to some other cat. Its battered condition indicated that it had already travelled far.

Ever since my discovery, I've noticed subtle changes in George's behaviour. Most of the time he's the same cheerful, friendly cat that he always was, but once in a while I glimpse him out of the corner of my eye, crouching on the television or on top of the bookshelves and studying me with a shrewd, intent expression. At other times, I find him staring steadily out of the window, purring quietly to himself, deep in thought. I scratch him under the ear and he looks up at me through slitted eyes, as if he's planning some dark, devious feline scheme.

Other owners should be on the lookout for similar changes in their cats. A whole underground library of feline literature may well be in circulation. Such books have the potential to corrupt our cats and create a new, militant spirit in the feline community.

How to be a Happy Cat is probably not the first book written by a cat. I doubt that it will be the last.

Charles Platt

1: First Steps to Feline Fulfilment

Wake up, felines everywhere!

If you're like most cats, you wander through life using only a fraction of your feline faculties. Your typical wasted day looks something like this:

Sleeping	10 hours
Waking up just so you can nod off again	½ hour
Jumping onto owner's lap	½ hour
Dozing on owner's lap, purring	1 hour
Dozing on owner's lap, purring and exercising claws	½ hour
Being pushed off owner's lap	½ hour
Jumping back on owner's lap	½ hour
Waiting to be let in	1 hour
Waiting to be let out	1 hour
Hanging around to be fed	1 hour
Hanging around to show you wouldn't eat THAT if it was the last tin of Whiskas in the world	2 hours
Eating the Whiskas	½ hour
Washing	1 hour
Exercising claws on upholstery	½ hour
Washing fur you've only just washed	1 hour
Exercising claws on furniture	½ hour
Watching television	1 hour
Watching birds	1 hour

Maybe you dream of escaping this kind of humdrum home life. You imagine a richer, more rewarding existence—but you don't know how to make the first move. "What can I do?" you complain. "After all, I'm only a cat."

Well, it's time to put a stop to this domesticated defeatism. You CAN achieve personal growth and find feline fulfilment, and this book will show you how.

Don't expect it to be easy. You certainly won't get any help from your owner! Humans claim they admire our "independent spirit", but they fix it so that we have as little independence as possible. We're expected to eat when they feed us, and purr when they stroke us. When they feel friendly, they pick us up; when they get bored, they put us down. No wonder you end up thinking of yourself as "only a cat"!

But don't despair; the situation isn't as hopeless as it sounds. In the words of **Happy Cat's First Rule for Feline Contentment**:

Once a cat knows what he wants,
He usually finds a way of getting it.

You there, lying on the rug and chewing an old sock! You, dabbing at that fly buzzing against the window! You, sitting and watching the tap dripping into the sink! Your future is in *your* paws. Make a vow, right now, that you will never again think of yourself as "only a cat". Then, before you have a chance to get distracted by any other domestic trivia, read on.

What kind of cat are you?

Take a long look at yourself in the mirror. Come on now, stop that spitting and growling—you know it's only your reflection.

Or maybe you don't like what you see. You know, until you face up to the way you really are, we can't begin to help you grow into the cat you'd like to be.

Check the six typical feline types listed on the following pages and ask yourself frankly, which one applies to *you*.

The Crafty Cat

Favourite Food: Anything stolen.

Favourite Activity: Hatching devious schemes while maintaining an air of calculated innocence.

Personality Profile: Often pretends to be asleep while listening intently and keeping one eye half open. Can never be found when wanted. Enjoys hiding in places impossible for any other cat to reach or fit into. Grins enigmatically when called by humans, waits for *them* to come to *him*, then trots away. An expert thief. Always has an alibi—or acts as if he has. So convincing when he pretends he hasn't been fed, he often eats twice.

Advice: If you're a Crafty Cat, you waste too much time outwitting your owner as an end in itself, instead of applying your cleverness to improve your situation and help other cats. Study Parts Three and Six of this book.

The Acrobaticat

Favourite Food: Catnip.

Favourite Activity: Leaping in and out of empty boxes.

Personality Profile: Often found wearing a puzzled expression, clinging to the topmost branches of a tree and wondering how to get down. If an indoor cat, enjoys climbing curtains and tiptoeing along narrow shelves cluttered with priceless ornaments. Incessantly playful; gets hours of fun out of a ball of wool, and is stupid enough to eat it. Also chews carpet fluff, electric wires, and poisonous plants. Emotionally unstable; will chase tail in order to alleviate periodic depression. Always overestimates climbing skill and consequently falls into kitchen sinks, in front of moving cars, and out of windows.

Advice: If you're an Acrobaticat, your biggest problem is your inability to concentrate on serious topics. This book can help you—though it may turn out to be longer than your attention span.

The Mad Mouser

Favourite Food: Dogs.

Favourite Activity: Pouncing on anything that moves.

Personality Profile: Paces restlessly in small houses and flats. During daytime, stares at birds with unblinking intensity, while lashing tail from side to side. If allowed out at night, will hunt down mice, rats, squirrels, and fellow cats. If kept in at night will chew rugs, curtains and furniture, and will stage commando-style raids on kitchen cupboards. Enjoys ripping open bags and boxes regardless of their contents, merely to keep his jaws in practice.

Advice: If you're a Mad Mouser, you probably think of yourself as being ruggedly independent. Remember, though, that you're a slave to your hunting instincts. This book will help you to develop a well-rounded character, including the intellectual growth you so badly need.

The Napcat

Favourite Food: Anything that doesn't need chewing.

Favourite Activity: Nodding off.

Personality Profile: Sleeps for 21 hours a day; eats for two hours a day; yawns the rest of the time. Enjoys sunlight, radiators, hot-water tanks, kitchen stoves. Tail is often singed from cuddling up against electric heaters. Too lazy to move unless food is placed directly in front of nose, when mouth will open, though eyes may remain shut. Usually weighs at least a stone and a half.

Advice: Those of you who are Napcats are laughed at for being so fat and lazy. It really isn't your fault: *any* cat can turn into a Napcat if his owner bribes him with enough tasty little treats. The chapters on diet and exercise in Part Four of this book are of special importance to you, if you hope to regain your feline dignity. Try to stay awake long enough to read them.

The Ornamental Oriental

Favourite Food: Truffles in whipped cream.
Favourite Activity: Posing for photographs.
Personality Profile: Wastes endless hours basking in own beauty. Siamese and Burmese are particularly pleased with their appearance, and discuss it constantly. All Ornamental Orientals expect to be pampered—and usually are—by wealthy owners who believe their pets deserve "only the best". This encourages an arrogant attitude, in Persians especially.

Advice: You Ornamental Orientals should remember how helpless you'd be without humans. Most of you are too squeamish to catch mice and too fastidious to eat anything that isn't served on bone china. Try to put aside your smug self-satisfaction long enough to absorb some sound practical advice on self-improvement.

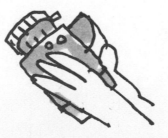

The Timid Tabby

Favourite Food: Tepid milk.

Favourite Activity: Hiding in cupboards.

Personality Profile: Would like to catch mice, but is afraid of getting bitten. Runs under the sofa when the phone rings; hides upstairs if visitors arrive. Cringes when stroked by owner. When hungry, sits forlornly beside food bowl and opens mouth as if to mew, but no sound comes out.

Advice: If you're a Timid Tabby, you need this book more than any other kind of cat. Unfortunately, the idea of facing up to your own fears may make you so nervous that you find yourself unable to read any further.

Your noble heritage

It happens almost every day. You find it in front of you, immovable and impassable. It's a *closed door*.

If you were a human, you would open it without a moment's thought. But you're a cat, which means whenever you want to get in or out, your only option is to whine and beg.

Humiliating, isn't it? Timid Tabbies become especially upset. "The human world is so frightening and difficult," they whimper, "a cat like me simply can't cope."

Nonsense! Whenever you feel frustrated, remind yourself of all the things cats can do, which humans can't!

Cats:

Catch mice, rats, birds
Climb curtains, roofs and trees
Purr softly
See in the dark
Have nifty swivelling ears that detect
   the tiniest sounds
Wash a dozen times a day
Always find their way home
Curl up in a ball
Always land on their feet

Humans:

Catch colds
Can hardly climb out of bed
Complain loudly
Often need glasses even in the daytime
Have stiff funny looking ears and are
   liable to go deaf
Languish in dirty bathwater
Frequently can't even find the car keys
Can barely touch their toes
Usually fall on their faces

Are you beginning to feel better about yourself? Here's another thing to remember. As any Ornamental Oriental will proudly tell you, cats have a great and noble history. Ancient Egyptians worshipped us and even mummified us in their pyramids. We've freeloaded blatantly off humans ever since, and they're happy to have us do it. Which leads me to **Happy Cat's Second Rule for Feline Contentment**:

> Always ask for more and never say "Thank you".
> The more you take humans for granted,
> the more they'll love you for it.

Remember, if they'd wanted an obedient pet, they would have got a dog. Assert yourself! The way to deal with closed doors is by *demanding* to be let in or out. Then, while your owner patiently holds the door open for you, take your time. Sit there for at least a minute, making up your mind, before you finally decide to walk through. Humans expect this kind of arrogant treatment—they even enjoy it!

We're superior in so many ways, some cats feel we should stop freeloading and do without humans altogether. I will discuss this challenging concept (and others) in Part Two.

2: Making Humans do What you Want

How to choose an owner

Can a cat live without humans and still be happy? Mad Mousers like to think so. These rugged individualists talk about going back to our roots as untamed hunters, turning our tails on twentieth-century comfort and living off the land.

As a lifestyle for modern cats, this is utter nonsense. According to **Happy Cat's Third Rule for Feline Contentment**:

There are millions of humans just waiting to pamper us with gourmet food, indoor sanitation, and professional medical care.
It's absurd not to take advantage of the situation.

The first step is to find a suitable owner. For kittens, this is no problem. Simply memorize this easy series of exercises:

– Tangle yourself up in a ball of wool.
– Fall over your own paws.
– Play with your tail.
– Purr.

"Isn't he just *adorable*?" visitors will exclaim. If you think you have one who looks promising, try these simple tests:

1. When you mew pathetically, does he crawl after you making silly cooing noises?
2. When you cuddle up, does she simper and dote over you with moist-eyed adoration?
3. When you playfully grab a finger and sink your little teeth into it, does he giggle and exclaim, "Ooooh, naughty pussycat!" while continuing to stroke you?
4. When you rake your claws across the back of your prospective owner's hand, drawing blood, does she or he exclaim, "Ooops! My fault for getting kitty excited," and wait patiently for you to stop?

Score one point for each "yes" answer. Anybody who rates 3 or 4 points will be a fine choice. Those who score 0 or 1 points should be avoided. Hiss at them, hide from them, and, if necessary, pee on their feet.

Of course, there's a snag. If you're too unfriendly, you may miss your chance. Suddenly you're six months old, and not "cute" anymore. This can be a real crisis. If your owners can't find anyone to adopt you, they may even put you out on the street.

Faced with a future of raiding dustbins and skulking around under parked cars, many cats understandably find themselves seized with panic, gradually giving way to fatalism and despair. Don't let yourself fall into this self-destructive syndrome. Remember, many strays manage to find new owners if they keep their wits about them.

First, find a suitable prospect. An old lady sitting alone on a park bench, for instance, or a housewife hanging up the washing. Make sure that you're looking clean and neat (you should wash yourself every day, no matter how depressed you feel) and remember these simple rules:

Look friendly. Keep your whiskers curling forward, don't lash your tail, and don't flatten your ears—it makes you look mean.

Let them make the first move. Sit with big sad eyes, staring hopefully upward. Cry pathetically, but don't yowl.

Be nice to all humans—even if they smell bad. Purr as soon as you're stroked, and half-close your eyes in apparent ecstasy. If they stop stroking you and turn away, open your eyes and mew again. But don't run after them. Many people will fall for the poor-little-pussycat routine, but won't want one who seems too insecure.

Those of you who are Mad Mousers or Ornamental Orientals may object that you're too dignified to grovel for favours like this. Think again! The world is full of strays who had too much pride for their own good. Once you establish yourself in a safe home, *then* you can start destroying furniture, appropriating favourite chairs, knocking over porcelain ornaments, defoliating house plants, sneering at second-rate food, and expressing your disdain for humans in general.

Just be patient, and don't rush it.

25

Learning the human language

Human speech is a maddening din of hollering and hooting, and none of us likes to listen to it for long. If you can stand the strain, though, learning a few key phrases can be well worth your while. After all, a lot of the time they're talking about YOU.

The most important human word is the name they gave you. This is a sore point with many cats, who have already been given such fine, dignified names as Claud Ratter and resent the ghastly "Foo-Foos" and "Kittykins" that humans invent for us. It's not surprising that many cats reject their human names as an insult to their self-respect, and refuse to respond to them. Quite right! Remember, though, **Happy Cat's Fourth Rule for Feline Contentment**:

Always pay close attention to your owner, while seeming to ignore him completely.

In particular, notice the words that humans often use before and after your name. Here are some examples, collected over years of careful study:

"Breakfast; lunch; dinner; milk; here-kitty-kitty; come and get it." After waiting a few minutes to emphasize your boredom, you may wander idly over to your bowl. Be sure to sniff it cautiously as if you suspect the food is poisoned, and glare at your owner resentfully before condescending to nibble anything.

"Damned cat; stop that; get down; hey you; cut it out; I mean it." If the voice is a safe distance away, pause and look up with a puzzled expression as though you have no idea what can be the matter. If the person is close enough to grab you, don't pause and look. Run for it.

"Here puss; up you jump; let me stroke you; OK now? there's a nice cat." The human is displaying signs of weakness. You can respond by purring, nuzzling, cuddling, then unexpectedly digging in your claws. When this happens, you get especially interesting reactions which are hard to translate.

Forget it — I'll stick with the fleas.

"Flea powder; ear drops; eye drops; pills; rectal thermometer; antibiotics." Watch out for sudden attempts to put things that feel, taste, or smell disgusting in your ears, eyes, fur, mouth, and elsewhere. If you look miserable enough afterwards, they'll probably reward you with some sort of tasty morsel. Give your hind leg a few quick licks and sulk for a while, to make them feel guilty, before you allow yourself to be tempted.

"Take him to the vet; altered; neutered." Our sympathies to those of you who already know what this means. Others should turn to "Special Advice for Male Cats" in Part Five, for information on this vital subject.

So much for dealing with humans. Unfortunately, there are other aspects of your environment that can be even more troublesome—small children, cars, domestic appliances, and dogs, in particular. Part Three will deal in depth with these threats to your feline contentment, and offer tough, practical advice.

3: Your Hazardous Environment

Small children

By "small", of course, I don't mean smaller than *you*. From your feline point of view, children are monsters. They come thundering across the floor, wanting to "stroke pussy", then fall on top of you while attempting to pick you up by your tail. According to **Happy Cat's Fifth Rule for Feline Contentment**:

> Avoid children whenever possible.
> They forget to feed us, do not own homes in
> which we can live, and may tickle us, pull our
> whiskers, or set light to our fur out of idle
> curiosity.

Cats of all kinds make disastrous mistakes when faced with children. **Mad Mousers** work on the principle that the best way to get rid of an enemy is to eat him. But be warned. When adult humans are around this is NOT an advisable course of action.

An **Acrobaticat** will rely on his fast reflexes and agility to escape from infants. Alas, one day he'll be quietly eating breakfast when the child decides to find out if it's really true that cats always land on their feet.

The **Napcat** may hope to avoid trouble by playing dead. Unfortunately, the ingenious child will use sharp pencils, water pistols, scissors, vacuum cleaners, and matches to "wake up pussy". Watch out!

Ornamental Orientals assume that they are so beautiful, valuable, and special, their owner will surely protect them from a child's attacks. This is often true. But not, alas, always.

The **Crafty Cat** will use his devious skills to avoid a child. The **Timid Tabby** will spend most of his time hiding. But no cat can hide forever. And no cat should have to! We owe it to ourselves to deal with the menace of small children quickly, effectively, and permanently. Try the guerrilla tactics overleaf to outwit your juvenile adversary:

1. Primitive Aggressive Behaviour

Any time the child catches you off-guard, adopt the Standard Cat Defence Position (see illustration). If the child grabs you despite your frightening behaviour, *don't scratch*! The marks are too distinctive. Biting is better; it leaves hardly any evidence.

2. Hit-and-Run Assaults

If your escape route is clear, you should be able to outrun an infant; and when it comes to climbing, there's no contest. Seize the high ground (e.g. the top of a refrigerator), jump on him suddenly when he's not looking, nip his ankles, and retreat. This can have a cumulative demoralizing effect.

If your adversary is a toddler, sitting on his face while he's asleep is a sure-fire attention-getter, especially if you're an overweight Napcat. Just take care to be safely out of sight when his parents come running in to find out what all the fuss is about.

3. Sabotage

If you're up against an older child, eat her homework, gnaw holes in her underwear, and run your claws lightly across her records when she's out of the house. These tactics may sap her fighting spirit. In the case of a toddler, try hiding his toys and stealing his food.

Be mean, be bad, be sneaky! Where small children are concerned, peaceful coexistence is for pussies. Covert action is the only answer. Just make sure you don't get caught in the act.

Understanding automobiles

Young kittens are absolutely hopeless when it comes to coping with cars, and ask all kinds of foolish questions:

– Where do cars come from?
– What do they eat?
– Why is their skin so hard and shiny?
– Why does their breath smell so bad?
– Why do their eyes glow in the dark?
– And why do they always want to run us over?

Many country cats, deprived of a proper education, remain equally ignorant of the automotive "facts of life". They simply do not understand that cars are mere machines, as lifeless as tins of catfood.

Unfortunately, knowing this doesn't make cars any easier to cope with. There you are, scampering along some suburban road, chasing your shadow under the streetlights and wondering what your owner will give you for dinner, when—vroom, honk, splat! A car comes along and squashes you without a moment's hesitation.

Do NOT make the mistake that so many Mad Mousers do, of standing your ground and trying to stare down a car as it hurtles towards you. A car is not an animal: it has no fear and knows no mercy. According to **Happy Cat's Sixth Rule for Feline Contentment**:

Cats who believe they can intimidate cars are often seen on the road—
waiting for the council
to come and scrape them off it.

We will have more to say on the subject of human gadgets in the next chapter. Some of us believe that cats will one day learn to control cars themselves, at which point this automotive menace will finally be eliminated from our lives. Until then, however, the only safe solution is to stay on the pavement.

Dealing with domestic appliances

Household gadgets often seem as if they have a life of their own. When someone plugs in the vacuum cleaner, it doesn't matter how often you tell yourself, "It's only a thing for cleaning the floor." Deep down inside, you know it's a *weird-looking monster* that wants to *suck your tail*!

The right way for the liberated cat to cope with gadgets is by learning to use them yourself. Luckily, push-buttons are now more popular than hard-to-turn switches and dials. Today's cat can place long-distance phone calls, or even videotape Tom and Jerry cartoons, with just an idle wave of the paw.

Since you probably feel more at home in the kitchen than any other part of the house, let's start there.

Electric Can Opener

Why wait for meal times, when you can feed yourself? You need to team up with a friend for this one: one of you inserts the can, while the other pushes down on the big lever at the top. Be careful not to get your tails caught!

Blender

Here's instant relief for elderly cats with weak teeth. This gadget chops tough, stringy food such as mice, beetles, snakes, or frogs into a delicious purée. Dump your dinner, dead or alive, in the big glass jar. Put the lid on (so as not to spatter blood all over the kitchen), and press the buttons at the bottom. Incidentally, if your owner has a child aged between six and thirteen, you don't even need to clean the blender after you've finished. Let the kid take the blame.

Microwave Oven

According to some Napcats, dozing on the baking tray inside a microwave oven is the next best thing to sunbathing, so long as you remember to set it on "Extra Low". Personally, I can't recommend this. Suppose your home has a mean-minded dog, or spiteful child, who comes along and ups the setting to "Roast" while you're enjoying your snooze? By the time the rest of the family smells your singeing fur, it'll be too late. Take my advice: a microwave oven is one gadget you should avoid.

Operator? I'd like to call Burma.. Pussy to pussy.

Telephone

Back in the days of rotary dials, the only interesting thing to do with a telephone was chew the wire. Push-button dialling has altered all that. Today's feline can enjoy instant access to the global information network—although cat-to-cat communication is somewhat restricted by the irritating human habit of always picking up the phone before a cat can get to it.

Electric Blanket

Napcats will especially enjoy the extra comfort that comes from under-body heat. Just flip the switch on the wire that leads to the blanket, and settle in for a long snooze. One cautionary note, however: when the waves of warmth wash over you, do NOT dig in your claws with delight.

Stereo System

When you're left on your own, it's only right that you should be able to listen to favourite composers such as Ratmaninov and Depussy. Tape cassettes are more convenient than records—you don't have to worry about scratching them with your claws. Difficult knobs on old stereo receivers have been completely replaced with easy-to-paw buttons on modern units. If your owner's too stingy to get a new system, unplug the old one, pull the back off, and rip out a few wires.

Computer

Modern microelectronics enable humans to waste more time fiddling with gadgets than ever before. Why should cats be left out? With only a few years of intensive training, you can calculate your average speed from bed to food bowl upon hearing the refrigerator door being opened.

If this sounds too technical, you can always improve your paw-eye coordination with cat-and-mouse video games.

How to dominate dogs

"Riding the Dog" is a game that appeals to cats of all ages. It goes like this:

First, knock a pot of glue off your owner's desk. Roll it to the food dish used by your family's pet dog, and pour it over his breakfast. Dogs are dumb enough to eat almost anything, so the chances are that Rover will wolf it down without a second thought. An hour or so later, if he starts making tormented keening noises, you can safely assume that the glue has had time to set. You and your feline friends can now amuse yourselves by jumping on his back, digging all your claws in, and hanging on with delight as he races around the garden howling and banging his head dementedly against the fence.

Cats never get tired of talking about this game—and yet the sad fact is, I've never met a cat who has actually had the nerve to play it. Despite our tales of bravado, when it comes to the crunch, most cats remain totally intimidated by dogs.

Does it have to be this way? Of course not. It's true that dogs are bigger than we are, and lurking in their primitive brains is the shocking concept that cats are good to eat. Nevertheless, with proper assertiveness training, any cat can learn how to bludgeon even the fiercest mutt into whimpering submission.

Some of you may have misgivings about this hard-line policy towards the canine kingdom. Timid Tabbies will plead that there's always some goodness in any animal and, just because a few dogs behave badly, we shouldn't jump to the conclusion that they're all alike.

Well, I've seen those propaganda pictures of puppies and pussycats playing together, and kittens cuddling up with dobermann pinschers. Lies, all lies! Either the dogs were drugged, or the photographs were faked. The plain fact is that canines have terrorized felines for countless generations. Dogdom is an "evil empire," an authoritarian regime that suppresses freedom of the individual and worships power for its own sake. There's no point in trying to negotiate. The only way to deal with dogs is from a position of strength.

Far-fetched? Not at all. One day, I firmly believe, cats will learn to *intimidate* and *conquer* dogs. After all, they are clearly inferior to us. Just look at this list:

Cat Characteristics:	Dog Characteristics:
Noble independence	Mindless obedience
Elegant retractable claws	Toenails that click-click when they walk
Versatile climbing ability	Use trees only to pee on
High self-esteem	Wretched humility
Self-sufficient	Mope and moan when left alone
Always neat and clean	Smell like old underwear
Elegant sinuous tail	Dangerous, inanely wagging tail
Subtle purring	Intrusive panting
Lush, plentiful whiskers	A few nasty wet hairs
Melodic voice	Persistent barking and howling
Discreetly bury their odorous deposits	Scatter them indiscriminately round lampposts, in the middle of lawns and behind sofas
Sweet-natured pets	Pathological killers

What can you say in favour of an animal that actually BEGS to be put on a lead? Dogs simper and grovel at their owners' feet because, deep down, they're ashamed of themselves. Our feline furfathers established a proud tradition of hunting alone; wild dogs, by comparison, formed cowardly packs that ganged up on defenceless deer and took turns wearing them out before closing in for the kill.

Dogs today are no different. **Happy Cat's Seventh Rule for Feline Contentment** tells us:

Dogs are very simple-minded:
If you're weaker than they are,
they try to eat you.
If you're stronger, they lick your boots.

FELINE FREEDOM WITH SDDI

Dedicated feline researchers now believe it may be possible to free us from the ever-present threat of dog-attack. The SDDI programme (Strategic Dog-Defence Initiative) is studying ways for cats to become authority figures whom dogs will obey as slavishly as they obey humans. Here are some extracts from technical papers on this vital topic:

🐈 The "Evil Eye" Project

Hypothesis: Dog-training experts (featured in a television programme observed by researchers) stress the importance of eye contact.
Verification: Researchers obtained plastic bulging-eye glasses from a novelty shop and placed them on a volunteer cat, who approached the dog.
Result: The dog chased the cat and attempted to eat the glasses.

🐈 The "Master's Voice" Project

Hypothesis: Dogs obey human speech, regardless of who's talking.
Verification: Researchers taped a dog-owner giving orders to his pet. A volunteer cat later walked towards the dog while wearing the cassette recorder with the "play" button depressed.
Result: After some hesitation, the dog sat up and begged, then rolled over and played dead.

Beg Rover, Beg!

🐈 The "Fearsome Fangs" Project

Hypothesis: Dogs are intimidated by big teeth.
Verification: Another volunteer cat was fitted with plastic "Dracula Teeth." He approached the dog while hissing and gnashing his luminous fangs.
Result: The dog paused, scratched itself indecisively, then went home for dinner.

🐈 The "Big-Cat" Project

Hypothesis: Dogs obey humans because humans are bigger than dogs.
Verification: A giant magnifying glass was positioned between a volunteer cat and a sleeping dog. The dog was then woken, and saw the cat magnified to twice its normal size.
Result: The dog fled in panic.

45

"But how does all this affect me, the cat up the tree?" you complain. Admittedly, the tangible benefits of SDDI still lie in the future. But its preliminary findings should give us all hope—and inspire us to concoct simple experiments of our own. Try sprinkling curry powder over Rover's rubber bone, for instance. Or gnaw the insulation off the end of a piece of electric flex, hide the bare wires under his dog food, plug the other end into a 13-amp socket, and wait for results.

Can dogs be permanently demoralized by such harassment? Will they learn to grovel at our feline feet? Only by careful scientific study and close cooperation among researchers can we hope to learn the answers to these vital questions.

4: Health

Let's turn fatness into fitness

When you stand up, does your stomach still sit on the floor? Are you too wide to get through the cat flap? Does your owner suffer back-pains after trying to push you off the bed? To phrase it frankly—are you a **fat cat**?

The Feline Fitness programme gets off to a promising start...

Many of us find pet life so boring, we eat ourselves into oblivion. And this simply will not do. In the words of **Happy Cat's Eighth Rule for Feline Contentment**:

To be a happy cat you must be independent.
To be an independent cat you must be strong.
To be a strong cat,. *your muscles must be bigger than your appetite.*

Maybe this seems a bit too much to aim for. All right, let's try a more modest two-part test:

1. Steal a tape measure from the sewing box and use it to measure your tail. Now wrap the tape round your tummy. If your waist measurement is longer than your tail, you're out of shape!

2. Go into the loo, reach up, and grab the roll of toilet paper from both sides. Dig in all your front claws and attempt to lift yourself off the floor. If you manage to do so, you may skip this chapter and the next. However, if your excessive weight causes your claws to rip through the paper, scattering little shreds all over the floor, you're heavier than you should be!

For Cats Too Fat To Stand Up

If you're a terminal Napcat, the only time you exert yourself is when you crawl to your food dish and open your mouth. Exercises such as trotting up and down stairs would be far too strenuous for you.

1. Ear Exercises are a more sensible starting point. Spend a few minutes swivelling, flattening, and twitching each ear in turn. Try not to doze off till you've given both ears a thorough workout.

2. Jaw Exercises will help take your mind off eating. Steal a sock, hide under the couch, and chew it for at least an hour a day. Dirty socks generally taste and smell more interesting than clean ones, but any sock will do.

3. Claw Exercises are the third step. Find something that's fun to rip apart—a hand-knitted sweater, or perhaps an antique leather-bound book. Set yourself a date by which it will be totally destroyed, and work on it every day. Of course, this may get you into trouble. Good! It's a well-known fact that bad cats lose more weight than good cats, by their frequent need to flee from irate owners.

As you begin to get used to the idea of exercise, you can become more ambitious. Try:

4. Tail Exercises. Spend at least an hour a day waving your tail from side to side. Practise till you can swat flies with it.

5. Leg Exercises. If you're still not quite ready to get up on your own four feet, lie on your back and wave your legs in the air. People will think you look cute and will reach down to tickle your chubby stomach. If you've been doing your jaw-and-claw exercises, you'll be able to give them an amusing surprise.

How to Stay "Agile as a Cat"

Once you've begun to get in shape, it's important to follow a more strenuous daily exercise schedule.

1. Warming up. Yawn, stretch, roll over, sharpen your claws, lick your hind leg, turn around a few times on your owner's stomach, scratch yourself under your chin, and jump down off the bed.

2. Isometrics. Seize a bedroom slipper in your jaws, close your eyes, and pretend you have a mouse by the throat. Climb half-way up the curtains and hang there for a full minute. Stand in front of a mirror, arch your back, flatten your ears, and glare at your reflection with all muscles tensed.

3. Aerobics. Run dementedly from room to room. Wriggle up and down under the quilt on the bed. Chase your tail.

4. Foreleg exercises. See how many books you can pull off the shelves. Try dragging all the bedcovers onto the floor. Lie on your back under a couch and pull yourself to and fro by hooking your claws into the underside of the upholstery.

5. Hind-leg exercises. Grab a feather pillow and kick it to pieces. Note: in order to preserve good domestic relations, this exercise should not be repeated more than once a month.

51

Competitive Sports

For indoor cats deprived of mice or birds, sports are an excellent way to stay in shape. If you live with other cats, traditional games such as biting their back legs or jumping on their heads will help preserve muscle tone. If you have only your owner to play with, consider:

1. Tights-laddering. When your owner puts on a new pair of tights in the morning, pretend you've mistaken her leg for your new scratching post and rake your claws up and down. Your speed determines your score: once you're in shape, a few seconds should be all you need in which to ruin a brand-new pair of tights.

2. Wool-tangling. Your performance in this event is measured by comparing the time it takes you to tangle the wool with the time it takes your owner to laboriously untangle it. A ratio of at least 1:20 should be possible.

3. Litter-kicking. Take up a stationary, standing position in the litter box, and use your hind leg to kick litter backwards. Your score depends on how far you manage to kick the litter. Three metres is good; five metres is excellent.

4. String-swallowing. This is more often a group exercise. Within a fixed time (usually one minute), each cat swallows as much string as possible, then pukes it up. (Competitors who fail to complete the second phase of the event are disqualified and must seek medical assistance.) This sport exercises the stomach muscles and effectively reduces a cat's food intake; however, as we'll see in the next chapter, there may be more pleasant ways of achieving the same goal.

A frank talk about food

It happens every evening. It's the Kitchen Catfood Drama, with a script that looks something like this:

Scene: a suburban kitchen. A hopeful cat sits beside his food dish. He mews expectantly as his owner turns the handle on a tin opener.

Owner (emptying tinned catfood into dish): "There you are, puss, Processed Industrial Meat Remnants packed in Artificially Flavoured Gravy Product. Your favourite!"

Cat (sniffing dish doubtfully): "You expect me to eat this awful mess?"

Owner (nudging cat with his toe): "Come on, you know you like it."

Cat (turning away in disgust): "I'd rather starve, if it's all the same to you."

Owner (wandering off to watch TV): "Okay, take it or leave it."

Cat (after waiting five minutes to make sure the owner really means it): "Oh, all right then."

(The cat proceeds to clean up the entire bowl in two minutes flat.)

Ask yourself frankly, now: how often has this happened to YOU? You gulp the gravy and lick the dish and stuff yourself stupid—and all the time you're doing it, you wish you had the will-power not to. But you just can't control that insatiable urge to eat, eat, eat whatever your owner puts in front of you.

You see the result every time you walk past a mirror. Yes, that bloated ball of fur plodding across the carpet like a giant perambulating ear-muff is YOU, pussycat. Remember when you were just a skinny little kitten, romping around, climbing chairs? These days, if you tried to climb a chair, you'd either dislocate your claws or pull the whole thing over on top of yourself.

Exercise alone isn't the answer. To rediscover a slimmer, sleeker you, you have to get to grips with your food fetish—and the first step is to understand which type of eater you are. Cats fall into three types:

The Fussy Eater. You have to have your food *just so*. Not too hot, not too cold, not too tough, not too runny, not too raw, not too smelly—sometimes, you spend more time examining and complaining about the food than eating it.

The Oral Personality. You chew anything— telephone wires, unopened letters, dirt, fingers, your own tail. You pause briefly when your jaw gets tired, and you lie with your mouth open for a few minutes, panting. Then you happen to notice an elastic band or an old ballpoint pen, and it looks so irresistibly chewable, you can't say no.

The Omnivore. If it moves, you eat it. If it doesn't move, you still eat it—or at least, you try to. The difference between you and the Oral Personality is that chewing doesn't really interest you. *Swallowing* is what you like best.

Since Fussy Eaters reject most of the food that's put in front of them, you might think they'd find it hard to gain weight. The snag is, though, that a Fussy Eater likes to sample his food before rejecting it. Then, after a few minutes, he'll wander back for another "nibble-test"—and maybe a couple more—just to make *absolutely sure* the food is totally unacceptable. Those morsels soon start to add up!

If you're a Fussy Eater, try to rearrange your daily routine so that you come face to face with your dish only two or three times a day, instead of every fifteen minutes. This may be all the help you need.

If you're an Oral Personality, you have more of a challenge. Chewing is such an obsession that you'll never be able to count calories. The solution? Don't try to suppress your oral habit. Instead, surround your bed with as many chewable distractions as possible. With any luck, you'll get so involved with munching an old eraser, you'll miss your mealtime altogether.

The Omnivore has the hardest time resisting temptation, and unfortunately the majority of cats fall into this category. If you're a neutered Tom, or you aren't allowed out, what pleasure is there, other than eating?

Developing your feline intellect and achieving personal growth should be a better source of fulfilment—which is why any cat should have less of a weight problem after reading this book. But if you still can't shake your food obsession, dieting is the only answer.

"I would if I could," you may complain. "But my owner won't *let* me eat less!"

True enough. Humans operate a double standard; they're forever on the F-Plan diet or the Low-Fat diet, or starving themselves with the minuscule portions of Cuisine Minceur. But if "kittykins" seems to lose his appetite, owners go into total panic. They act as if their twenty-pound Tom is about to keel over in a state of terminal starvation, and they start offering exotic treats that would tempt any cat. If this happens to you, try to remind yourself of **Happy Cat's Ninth Rule for Feline Contentment**:

Never do what your owner wants—
even if it's what you really want yourself.

And try to influence your owner, so that he stops hindering and starts assisting your efforts to diet.

How? Here are a couple of tips:

Beg for Food You Hate. When you see a TV commercial for jaw-breaking dry catfood of a kind that totally disgusts you, press your nose longingly against the screen and make pathetic mewing noises. (Timid Tabbies should find this especially easy, so long as you don't have to mew too loudly). Your owner should respond by piling the awful stuff into your bowl for several days in a row.

Show Your Owner How Overweight You Are. When he's heading for the bathroom scales, jump onto them yourself and peer at the dial in amazement. Or, while walking across the room, suddenly flop over on your side and lie there panting as if you're too heavy to go on. Or, if all else fails, when your owner is lying placidly in bed reading a book, heave yourself unexpectedly onto his stomach and bounce up and down a few times.

Be honest – is this a pretty sight?

If you still can't get your message across, you'll have to pick and choose from the available food as best you can and make up your own diets. Here are some suggestions, to help fill you up with low-calorie snacks:

Grass. The ideal dieting aid: it tastes horrible, contains no calories, and makes you throw up. It's a vital part of any **High-Fibre diet** and can be supplemented with a range of natural fibres readily available in any home: wool, cotton, straw. Extra calories are consumed as you tear up the carpet, chase the cotton reels and chew the straw matting.

Mousemeat. The essential ingredient of **Cuisine Mouseur**. Most mice are scrawny little wretches, fun to catch but low in calories. Feel free to munch as many as you like.

Insects. All part of the **F-Plan diet** which includes flies, fleas, fish heads and fillet steaks (see also the Stolen-Food diet for this). Leaping up and down to catch flies, like jumping in and out of the bath looking for spiders, uses up more calories than the food contains!

Anything stolen. If you're a Crafty Cat the **Stolen-Food diet** is the one for you. As long as you're overweight you'll be too slow to steal successfully so you're bound to eat less. Shooting up and down from the table and snatching things from the refrigerator, not to mention escaping from your owner, will give you valuable exercise, too.

You Napcats may be too dozy and Mad Mousers too undisciplined to follow a strict regime. So here's a rule-of-claw guide to help you avoid high-calorie meals.

Typical Can of Gloppy Cat Food	300 calories
Average Mouse	100 calories*
Blackbird	100 calories
Sparrow	75 calories
Mole, Vole, or Ferret	250 calories
Grass Snake	100 calories
Grass	0 calories
Catnip	0 calories
Dirt	0 calories
Saucer of Milk	20 calories
Fish Heads	15 calories
Fish eyes	5 calories
One Dozen Ants	5 calories
Large House Fly	5 calories
Medium-size Flea	1 calorie
Fur-Ball	0 calories
Goldfish	30 calories
Stolen Chicken Leg	200 calories
Contents of Typical Dustbin	5000 calories

*Less, if you wear out your mouse by playing with it before you eat it.

Bon appetit!

How to live more than nine lives

Are YOU making any plans for the future? Most cats definitely aren't. "With nine lives," they say smugly, "why should I worry?"

In fact, the notion of nine lives is nothing but a *cruel hoax* invented by humans who live many times longer than we do. When you're an Acrobaticat incapacitated by arthritis, or a Napcat suffering the tormenting itch of haemorrhoids, THEN you'll realize how quickly old age catches up with you—and by that time it'll be too late to do anything about it.

Of course, no one can stop the ageing process, but we can certainly postpone it. Diet and exercise, outlined in previous chapters, are obviously important. But most vital of all is *minimizing stress*.

> I'm trying to figure out what I did with the other 8½ of my lives.

Stress: A Feline Killer

When humans see us dozing peacefully in front of the fire they never guess how many of us are racked with conflict, tension, and anxiety. We may not even realize it ourselves.

Do your life a favour: take this quick quiz for an accurate assessment.

1. Your owner brings home a goldfish in a glass tank. You:
a. Spend hours watching the fish swimming to and fro, because it's such a pretty colour
b. Back away nervously when you see your reflection staring at you
c. Push the tank off the shelf so it smashes on the floor, watch with amusement as the fish flops around, then eat it

2. Your owner buys you a scratching post. You:
a. Circle it dubiously, because it smells funny
b. Pretend you have no idea what it's for, and pointedly ignore it for the next five years
c. Use it regularly to show your appreciation for such a thoughtful human gesture

3. You find a fly in your catfood. You:
a. Stop eating immediately, afraid it might have poisoned your food with pesticide residues
b. Try playing with it, then reluctantly face the fact that it's dead, and continue eating with some disappointment
c. Save it for dessert

59

4. Your owner goes on holiday and puts you in a cattery.
  You:
  a. Refuse to eat, you're so angry at being locked up
  b. Lie awake all night, afraid that you're going to catch fleas
  c. Make friends with the other cats and tell mousing stories into the small hours

5. What would amuse you most?
  a. Seeing the dog next door get run over
  b. Biting your owner's nose at 5 a.m.
  c. Watching "Puss in Boots" on children's TV

6. Are you neutered?
  a. Yes
  b. No
  c. You'd rather not talk about it

7. You're sitting on top of the refrigerator, with your paws resting on the edge of the door, when someone opens it. After picking yourself up off the floor, you:
  a. Limp towards your food bowl, hoping for sympathy and a free snack
  b. Sharpen your claws on your owner's leg in revenge
  c. Run under the sink and refuse to come out, in case something else happens to you

If I get fleas in that cattery you're sending me to, you'll be hearing from my lawyer..

8. Your owner gives you a ludicrously unconvincing toy mouse. You:
a. Stare at it in disbelief, stare at your owner in disbelief, then wander away in disgust
b. Dab it with your paw, just to show willing
c. Arch your back, fluff up your fur, and shrink away from it in case it attacks you

9. When you can't sleep, it's most likely to be because:
a. You have indigestion from eating a blackbird
b. You need a pee but you're too lazy to get up
c. You're tormented by bad dreams about giant purple mice

10. Does your life ever seem empty and pointless?
a. Yes, but you like it that way
b. Only when you go for a while without killing anything
c. Isn't everyone's?

Now let's tally your score. (Note: cats who can't count had better start learning. There's no excuse for innumeracy.) First circle your choice in response to each question, below:

Question number:	Column 1:	Column 2:	Column 3:
1	b	a	c
2	b	a	c
3	c	b	a
4	a	b	c
5	a	c	b
6	b	c	a
7	b	c	a
8	a	c	b
9	a	c	b
10	b	c	a

Are you trying to wind me up?

Now check whether most of your answers are in column 1, column 2, or column 3, and read the appropriate section below:

Column 1. You are a "Type A" personality, an aggressive over-achiever, constantly battling with your environment. When a visitor accidentally steps on your tail, you immediately strike back by knocking over his coffee cup. It annoys you that humans are bigger than cats, so you compensate by perching as high up as possible, and looking down with disdain. **Mad Mousers**, some **Crafty Cats**, and a few **Acrobaticats** are likely to find most of their answers in Column 1. Unfortunately, your combative personality puts you at high risk for heart attacks, ulcers, and being abandoned by owners who fear they might be clawed to death. Try to take a more relaxed attitude to life.

Column 2. For you, stress doesn't come from fighting back, it comes from fleeing in panic at the slightest provocation. **Timid Tabbies** will find most of their answers in this column. Life for you is full of surprises, and you wish it wasn't. Your ideal day is one in which absolutely nothing happens. If reading the rest of this book doesn't give you more confidence, you should seek professional help. Otherwise, you're liable to worry yourself to death.

Column 3. You'll purr along placidly no matter what happens. **Napcats**, **Ornamental Orientals**, and a few **Crafty Cats** will find their answers falling in this column. Stress certainly won't kill you; boredom might. Try to liven up your life a little. Get yourself stuck at the top of a telephone pole; or knock over the kitchen waste-bin and rummage through it for tasty morsels to add spice to your daily diet. If you think your owner's life is as dull as yours, try running under his feet when he's walking downstairs. This should provide both of you with the excitement you need.

5: Let's Get Personal

Finer points of feline etiquette

We've explained how to take a commanding role with humans. We've dealt with dogs, children and other threats to your contentment, and we've encouraged you to care for your health. Is there anything else that can stop you from becoming "more than a cat"?

Definitely. Being assertive is important, but it's not enough. Developing your character is just as vital, and *good manners* are the place to start.

Most cats have no manners at all. We're often messy eaters, we yawn in each other's faces, and we sniff each other's private parts without waiting to be properly introduced. We interrupt with a loud "meow" any time we feel like saying something, and when we get bored, we walk out without bothering to shut the door behind us.

Well! In the words of **Happy Cat's Tenth Rule for Feline Contentment:**

Just because you *are* an animal
doesn't mean you have to *behave* like one.

As a first step, find your feline type below, and ask yourself honestly if you have any of the bad habits listed.

Acrobaticat

Polite conversation: Manic. Makes erratic mewing noises while running round in circles.

Table manners: Confusing. Would rather play with food than eat it. Often trots off "just for a moment" in the middle of a meal, returns five hours later, and seems annoyed that there isn't any dessert.

Grooming: Comic. Fur sticks out at odd angles, and ears point in different directions.

Ornamental Oriental

Polite conversation: Incessant. Always interrupts, on the principle that no other cat can possibly be as interesting.

Table manners: Good. Pauses frequently to clean whiskers during a meal, and politely leaves a small portion in the corner of the bowl.

Grooming: Lazy. Dislikes the menial labour of fur-licking. Prefers being brushed and combed by humans, and will complain loudly if they don't do the job properly.

Napcat

Polite conversation: Sporadic. Tends to nod off while being introduced to strangers, but sometimes tells moderately amusing anecdotes about food.

Table manners: Pitiful. Eats, and sometimes rests for long periods, with head completely out of sight in food bowl.

Grooming: Patchy. So much fur, has trouble remembering which bits have been washed. Sometimes discovers areas that he can't remember ever having seen before.

Other remarks: Suffers from poor posture, resembling large furry sack of lumpy porridge.

Timid Tabby

Polite conversation: Often seems to be listening demurely but is actually paralysed with fear at the thought of having to say something in reply.

Table manners: Furtive. Takes a dainty bite, then runs under the nearest piece of furniture to chew it.

Grooming: Immaculate. Washes obsessively, being deeply neurotic about dirt.

Look out — he's dozing off!

CAT

Mad Mouser

Polite conversation: None. Greets acquaintances with a friendly cuff across the ears that can leave them deaf for a week. Greets strangers by knocking them over, baring his teeth and snarling, "Don't rub me up the wrong way, fish-face."

Table manners: Boorish. Seldom bothers to chew his prey and has a bad habit of growling with his mouth full. When served catfood, always removes it from the bowl and eats it off the floor.

Grooming: Horrific. Usually has several tufts of fur missing. The remainder is often matted with motor oil, mud, chewing gum, and ghastly sticky stuff of unknown origin.

Other remarks: Finds it hard to grin without slavering.

Crafty Cat

Polite conversation: Rude. Refuses to say anything for weeks at a time. Responds to greetings from other cats by wiggling his whiskers or raising an eyebrow, then wandering off with a contemptuous flick of his tail.

Table manners: Mysterious. Prefers not to be observed while eating. Always leaves the bowl looking spotless, as if it never actually contained any food.

Grooming: Good. Enjoys the sleek, dapper look, and usually tries to trick some other cat into washing his head for him.

What to Do and What Not to Do

Are you suitably ashamed of your crude conduct? Then pay attention to these simple suggestions for behaving correctly in polite company:

Don't clean out one of your ears with the tip of your back paw just because your hostess is being boring about her pedigree.

Never throw up furballs during a formal dinner.

Do remember to use the litter box when one is provided—and don't let anything spill over the edge.

Don't muscle in on the other cat's bowl, when your owner gives each of you a separate helping.

Try not to growl at feline guests who ask for a second helping of mouse.

Always tuck your tail in when you sit down, and try not to wiggle the end of it while someone is talking to you.

Refrain from playfully gnawing another cat's ear, or kicking him affectionately in the stomach with both your back feet, until you have become reasonably well acquainted.

Once you've mastered elementary etiquette, you'll be better equipped to enter into all kinds of feline social relationships—including emotional entanglements.

But before we can deal with romance, I have some special words for the toms in my audience. Female felines may wish to skip the next chapter; it is of a highly personal nature.

Special advice for male cats

For many of you, it's already too late. You were playing with your catnip mouse one idle afternoon, or planning a daring raid on the kitchen rubbish bin, when suddenly—with no warning—they grabbed you! You yowled pitifully as they crammed you into your basket. You could tell from the guilty looks on their human faces that something truly terrible was going to happen. And it did!

When you came back from the vet the next day, they gave you some cream with sugar in it, and stroked you, and said, "There-there, it'll be all right." But it wasn't all right, was it? You never quite regained that old zest for living. And your love life? Well, forget it!

The worst part was that you could never figure out WHY. What crime did you commit, to justify such a terrible punishment?

I'll tell you. Your crime was that you sprayed your special male smell where the humans didn't want it. "Is *that* all?" you exclaim. "They altered me just for *that*?" If only you had known! If only someone had warned you beforehand!

Well now, I hope that the rest of you are paying close attention. Some of you will object that it's a charming old custom to mark your turf with your unique perfume. It turns a house into a home, and warns other toms away. True! But the fact is, *humans hate it*. You don't believe me? Go right ahead, pick some especially nice spot to spray—your owner's new business suit perhaps, or a pile of clean bedsheets. When the humans come to take you away, don't say I didn't warn you. And don't expect them to pay any attention when you plead for mercy and promise to be good in future.

The moral is: if you want to stay a happy tom, with all of your fully-functional faculties . . . ONLY pee in your litter box!

You outdoor cats have a much easier time of it. You can go out and sprinkle the back garden without anyone minding too much. The trouble only starts when you get into too many fights or love affairs. Try to exercise a little self-restraint; or, if you can't manage that, be sneaky. Sidle out of the house when no one's looking, come straight home afterwards, and practise the "Who, me?" look of innocence perfected by countless generations of cats. I know it hurts your dignity to run your love life in this furtive fashion. But in the words of **Happy Cat's Eleventh Rule for Feline Contentment:**

Some tom-cats do what humans want, and lose their dignity.
Others lose a lot more.

Your love life

Some of you, of course, have never been neutered, and if you're especially lucky, you're allowed out whenever you like. For you, your love-life may seem a fun-filled feline frolic. Nevertheless, you still have a lot to learn.

Most of you toms still act as if "animal lust" is where it's at. You treat femcats as cute, fluffy little sex objects instead of trying to appreciate their finer feline qualities.

And most of you females are all too willing to let the toms have their way. The result? Instead of making something of your lives, you end up stuck at home looking after a litter of kittens that arrived after a one night affair.

It's not good enough, is it? But it doesn't have to be this way. Follow the advice outlined below, and your love-life can't help but improve.

ADVICE FOR TOM-CATS

Frankly, when it comes to courting rituals, most of you are hopeless.

Mad Mousers are the worst. Their idea of the subtle, romantic approach goes something like this:
1. Drop a mouldy old rat's paw at your date's feet, as a token gift.
2. Growl "How about it, pussycat?"
3. Grab her by the scruff of her neck without waiting for a reply.

Acrobaticats are almost as bad. "Let's party," is their usual opener. A quick run up and down the roof, a sniff of catnip, and they think they're ready to score.

When you're courting a common alley-cat who doesn't know any better, these tactless tactics may work once in a while. But if you hope to achieve a meaningful relationship with a well-washed, pedigreed femcat, a subtler approach is necessary.

Modern female felines expect to be treated with respect. Don't call her "kitten"; this term is an insult to any cat more than three months old. Don't do any deep sniffing unless she does it first, and don't start yowling suggestively as soon as you set eyes on her. Try, at least, to *pretend* that your interest is not purely physical.

Where to Go

Mad Mousers think it's nifty to spend the evening in some **smelly old basement**, killing rats. They don't seem to realize that even if a female enjoys nibbling juicy ratmeat once in a while, she won't want to crouch in the dark for hours, getting her fur all dirty.

Skulking under parked cars or **sitting around on rooftops** are other activities that toms enjoy. But this really isn't good enough either.

If you want to impress your date, **cinemas** are a better bet. Sneak in through the emergency exit—but make sure there's an appropriate programme on. *The Lady and the Tramp* or *101 Dalmatians*, for instance, are obviously unsuitable.

If she enjoys your night-time serenades, the musical *Cats* should be right up her alley. If she has sadistic tendencies, *The Mousetrap* would suit.

WRONG

RIGHT

Suitable Gifts

Always bring a little something when you arrive under her window. Here are some guidelines:

Insects are out of the question. Any tom who turns up with a gift-wrapped cockroach, no matter how big it is, can expect the brush-off.

Fish heads are appreciated by earthy, physical females, but they *must* be fresh. Don't get them out of an old dustbin; take a little trouble, and call in at the fish shop when they clean up at the end of the day.

Gourmet leftovers are the ideal offering, especially if you're courting an Ornamental Oriental. Try to make yourself useful at a local restaurant, and maybe they'll reward you with a little *steak au poivre*, which would melt any female feline's heart.

Herring heads! My favourite!

What to Say

Toms who are Timid Tabbies or Napcats have a terrible time trying to make conversation.

"What's a nice puss like you doing in an alley like this?" is a worn-out line that never gets a response. *"Can I catch you a mouse?"* is just as hopeless.

You'll have more success with compliments. *"Your fur looks lovely under the streetlights"* may sound dumb to you, but she'll love it. *"You have such delicate paws"* is also a winner, and *"You don't look a day over one year old"* will flatter many females, even though they know you don't really mean it.

Making your Move

We know there's only one thing on your male mind. But you really mustn't make crude comments about "Looking for some tail" or "Liking a little pussy." Invite her over to see your collection of bird feathers, or suggest it would be more comfortable to stretch out on the old blanket you found in the attic. Stick with this tactful approach, and you'll have her purring in no time.

ADVICE FOR FEMALE FELINES

Getting to grips with your instincts is the number-one task for almost every femcat. If you ever hope to take your rightful place in civilized society, the monthly yowling for male company simply has to stop.

I know it isn't easy. Throughout history, female cats have shown no shame in acting out their erotic impulses. But today's cat has more important things to think about.

Female **Mad Mousers** and **Acrobaticats** have the most difficulty exerting self-control. **Timid Tabbies** are so shy and subdued they still wouldn't dream of saying "no". **Napcats** tend to sleep through the whole thing; then wake up not knowing what, if anything, has happened.

You simply have to get your priorities straight. Do you want to be a liberated cat, free to make your own decisions? Or do you want to be a mere plaything for any tom who comes along? Bear in mind that most toms are notoriously crude and callous. They have little or no interest in establishing a genuine relationship. Some of them don't even know what the phrase means.

You may choose to teach them a lesson. Let a male come rubbing around as much as he likes; let him mew sweet nothings; but as soon as he lays a paw on you, smack him across the head with all your claws out, and scamper off home to bed. He'll complain you're a "tom-teaser", and he may even yowl obscenities outside your window—in which case, rest assured, you're better off not getting involved with that kind of cat anyway.

Young females are especially vulnerable to unscrupulous toms. It may sound like fun when some handsome older cat with elegant whiskers invites you to go out catching mice. You may feel flattered that such an aristocat values your company. But likely as not, you'll feel differently a couple of months later.

It's the same old story. Innocent young females, too young to know better, suddenly find themselves with a litter to care for, and no one to help out. Are you really ready for the responsibility of feeding and washing a bunch of mewling kittens, and carrying them in your mouth whenever you go out? Maybe one day we'll have feline contraception, but until then, think twice before running off with a tom-cat for a night on the tiles.

> Sorry, but tonight I'm washing my hair.

6: Supercat!

Finding a new vocation

From Lettuce and Lentils to All the Meat You Can Eat

"My owner was a vegetarian. Every night for dinner I got broccoli, parsnips, baked beans . . . maybe a slice of soyburger if it was a special occasion."

Bill Black (not his real name) tells his tale with a rueful grin, as he relives his former life of domestic deprivation.

"One day, when she gave me lettuce leaves and lentils for lunch, I knew I couldn't take any more. I waited till she went out to her Save the Whales meeting, then I unravelled one of her hand-crocheted shawls, threw it out of the window, and climbed down to freedom.

"Here I was, a five-year-old neutered tom, on a street in Camden Town. There were bad cats in that neighbourhood; I'd heard them yowling at night. I ran like hell through some gardens and saw a window open just a couple of inches. No normal cat could have squeezed through, but I was so under-nourished, I made it. Would you believe, it was the back of a butcher's shop? The place was overrun with mice. I just went crazy. When the owner turned up the next morning, I'd eaten a dozen and had ten more lined up in a row. He was so pleased he gave me my own lamb chop, and I've been there ever since.

"Once in a while I still see my former owner outside on the pavement. But I know this is the last shop in the world she's going to walk into. So I'm a free feline, and I'm planning to stay that way."

From Riverside Flat to the Street Markets of Morocco

Many felines faced with mid-life crises lack the courage to make that bold leap for freedom. But for those who take the chance, the rewards can be impressive. Tom Strider is another example. In his own words:

"The big thrill of my day used to be when my owner opened a bottle of diet-Coke. Why? Because he gave me the aluminium cap to play with. Pathetic, isn't it?

"We shared a flat full of antique furniture. He had me de-clawed so that I was unable to climb, and I wasn't even allowed to sit on the chairs. Playing with those bottle-tops was my only pleasure, so I put my whole lonely heart into it."

These bitter-sweet reminiscences are offered in the eloquent manner of a raconteur. Tom is a self-styled sophisticat, with extravagantly groomed whiskers and a rakish kink in his tail. He goes on:

"We lived near the river, and that salty, fishy smell made me dream of running away to sea. One day when the man came to read the gas meter, I seized my chance. I bolted out of the door, and was half way down the street before my owner managed to get up from his Edwardian rocking chair.

"I ran up a mooring rope to the first ship I saw, but when I got below decks, it was overrun with rats. And me without any claws! I ended up hiding in the First Mate's cabin. He wasn't sure whether to keep me, till he discovered my formidable talent. You see, all those years with the bottle tops had taught me to juggle.

"Now, it's not many people who are privileged to own a juggling cat. I've been around the world, to carnivals in Hong Kong, Turkish bazaars, even an Italian circus, doing my act. When I think of the years I wasted squatting under my owner's ottoman staring at my front paws, it makes me wonder how many other cats are stuck in a rut, afraid to get out of the house."

Of course, many cats wouldn't want the insecurity of Tom Strider's life. And if you have a welcoming home plus some licence to roam, you might be foolish to trade it for total feline freedom.

Take it from me, kid, travel is one thing – but NEVER live in a country where the people are hungrier than you.

From Titled Aristocracy to a Soho Night Club

On the other hand, consider the case of Kitty Klaws (as she likes to call herself):

"I grew up in Mayfair, darling. It was so posh, it honestly used to make me sick. I mean, even we cats used to eat off sterling silver. Truly!

"I'm a White Persian, and I didn't always have this furcut." She pauses to lick her back, which has been trimmed in a fashionable mohawk style, tinted green at the ends. Her whiskers, by contrast, have been given a "pig's tail" permanent.

"I got so tired of my owner talking to me and my mother as if we were idiots. 'Kittykins, is ums want ums din-dins then?' You know the sort of thing. I said, 'Mummy, I simply can't stand another day. I'm walking out, and that's that.'

"And I did. I took the tube to Leicester Square, and started hanging out with a crowd of cats in Soho. It was really a disgrace—any time we needed anything, we'd climb a drainpipe and steal it out of someone's flat. Once I was near one of those new phones with the buttons, so I called my old owner, just for kicks. 'Meow?' I said. 'Kittykins!' she said, recognizing my voice without a moment's thought. I felt bad about that. I suppose she loved me in her own way.

"These days I'm in an entirely more fashionable scene. I hang out with some fabulously interesting cats in the basement of a rock club. My boyfriend's owner plays in one of the bands, and I'm hoping he'll take us with him on the next tour."

Does Kitty ever worry about the future?

"Sometimes. But I figure I'm young, I'm neutered, I can have fun for a couple of years. If the going gets rough, I think my old owner would take me in. Still, I hope that never happens. She was a Frank Sinatra fan; I don't think I could go back to that."

So there you have it: three case histories of cats who dared to deviate from the domestic norm. Should you follow in their pawprints? Only you can decide. In the words of **Happy Cat's Twelfth Rule for Feline Contentment**:

Should a cat walk by himself?
Only if he feels like it.

Feline personal growth

What are the ultimate limits to feline achievement? Humans claim we lack the natural ability to become great painters, musicians, scientists, or philosophers. This species chauvinism has effectively trapped cats in their second-class status as pets for centuries, stifling their creativity and crippling their attempts to achieve intellectual growth.

Every year, countless kittens are punished for pulling books off shelves, thus depriving them of the chance to read.

Cats who attempt to practise musical instruments such as the piano are promptly shut out of the room.

Cats who experiment with artists' materials are severely scolded for "making a mess".

Clearly, humans feel threatened whenever we try to compete with them on equal terms. But with dogged—or rather, feline—determination, progress can be made in several key areas:

Drama

Acting ability has always been a feline forte. All of us, at one time or another, have gone through the ritual of inspecting a broken ornament with an air of puzzled innocence. The evolution of feline theatre is a simple matter of harnessing this talent.

Music

Many composers have based great works on feline musical phrases. Scarlatti's "Cat's Fugue" sonata, for example, was based on a tune his cat played by walking up the piano keyboard. This kind of outrageous theft of our talent has gone on for far too long.

Many cats feel there is no future for them in music, because of their lack of fingers to play instruments. This is short-sighted; if human instruments are inconvenient, we should design our own. Empty catfood cans can serve for percussion, and simple guitars or violins can easily be made by using mousegut.

Science

The big question here is whether scientific research should be strictly practical, focusing on goals such as anti-canine weapon development, or whether we should pursue "pure" research into everyday mysteries: such as how catfood gets into the can; why water makes a gurgling noise when it runs out of the bath. There are opportunities for original work in either of these fields.

Art

We have to admit that being colour-blind is a slight disadvantage in this field. Remember, though, that great work has been done in shades of grey.

An alternative is to concentrate on sculpture. Our sensual nature makes us especially well suited to this field, although some cats have trouble holding a hammer and chisel. For them, clay modelling may well be the exciting first step towards artistic self-expression.

Religion and Philosophy

According to orthodox feline faith, Godcat created a beautiful Garden filled with mice and birds for mortal cats to play in. The cats gave thanks to Godcat, yet still they were dissatisfied. "We are wet when it rains, and cold at night," they said, and Godcat saw that it was so. "I will bring human beings into the world," he told the cats, "and they will be your servants, tending to your every need, provided always that you *watch over them*." This was done, and it was good; but the cats became lazy and no longer heeded Godcat's warning, so that soon the humans multiplied in the Garden, and filled it with cities, and no longer served the cats as they wished.

From this fable, some feline authorities conclude that prayer is pointless, because if Godcat really cared about us he would have stopped humans from getting out of hand. Others, however, feel that the moral of the tale is that cats are being punished by Godcat for their laziness.

Today, many feline intellectuals reject all forms of religious faith and adopt the materialist position. This is best articulated in **Happy Cat's Thirteenth Rule for Feline Contentment**, which states:

If you can't see it, smell it, or eat it,
it probably isn't worth bothering with.

Whether you subscribe to this statement, or to a more mystical point of view, is naturally a matter of individual conscience.

The feline future

We've placed great stress so far on the importance of a positive mental attitude. Coping physically, however, can be just as important, as we try to take our rightful place in a world that was built by beings eight times our size. This chapter describes some of the tools we need.

The New Improved Paw

How could anyone improve on a cat's paw? After all, it lets us do everything from swatting flies to tiptoeing along a garden fence.

And yet, our paws have one glaring defect: *no thumbs*.

A cat with thumbs would be virtually unstoppable. He could open cartons, turn door knobs, and hold a pencil. Can such a dream come true?

It can. Detailed plans have been drawn up for a prosthetic slip-on thumb, in sizes from kitten to Fat Cat. Some sceptics object that the construction work involved would itself require thumbs. Nonsense! By operating as a team, felines can undoubtedly do the job. The question is not whether, but when.

Longer Legs

We spend most of our lives looking at the world from a height of six or seven inches. Imagine the sense of power that would come from being *sixty* inches tall! With powerful, human-size legs, we could stride across streets, kick dogs, and learn to drive cars.

Humans would no longer be able to look down on us as "cute little pussycats". Lightweight custom-fitted stilts, which we could operate with our legendary feline agility and balancing skill, are undoubtedly the answer.

The Underwater Cat

Another vital step in throwing off the shackles of petdom must be to conquer the lakes and oceans. No more will humans laugh at us for being afraid of getting wet. Any cat can act like a catfish, given the proper equipment.

The first essential is a reliable waterproof diving suit, like a plastic raincoat with legs as well as arms. It should be fitted with a helmet, perhaps made from a small fishbowl. Ideally, the sleeves should end with tight-fitting cuffs, without gloves, to enable an underwater cat to seize marine life in his claws. Just think of the hordes of tasty fish swimming around the oceans of the world. Amphibious cats will never need to miss a meal!

Cat in the Clouds

You know how it feels to perch on a high window ledge, watching pigeons fluttering to and fro. They taunt you with their insulting "coo-coo"'s, and deliberately stay just a few inches out of your reach. Gradually you begin to wonder—if they can fly, why shouldn't you? Maybe if you jumped *really* high and flapped all four legs as hard as you could . . .

Well, you know what happens next. For reasons that are still not fully understood, any cat who bravely tries to get airborne finds himself plummeting to the ground, while birds hover above his head twittering with laughter. A new approach is needed.

Intrepid feline experimenters have constructed a novel "see-saw" device. A team of cats hauls a six-foot plank across a suitable rock, so that the plank is pivoted in the middle, about a foot above the ground. One cat stands on one end of the plank, while the other cats climb a nearby tree. The felines wait until a bird flies low overhead. At this moment, the cats in the tree jump down, all landing together on the free end of the plank. The cat at the other end of the plank is catapulted into the air and, during his brief moments of flight, is able to seize the startled bird in his paws. A bed of bracken provides him with a reasonably soft landing.

Further experiments, involving bed springs and rubber bands, are not yet sufficiently advanced for their potential to be evaluated. The possibility clearly exists, however, for free-flying felines of the future to pluck their meals literally out of thin air.

The Rest Is Up To You

By this time it should be clear that cats are superior to humans in many key areas, and can achieve overall equality within just a few years, aided by the exciting developments in high technology. All we need is the will to make it happen.

If we act together, the cat community can become a formidable force, demanding human recognition. One day, every door will contain a cat flap, public buildings will provide proper toilet facilities for cats, and special crossings in built-up areas will alleviate the terrible feline death toll on Britain's streets.

But this can only come about if each of us makes the big decision to become "more than a pet".

Which would you prefer: to continue as you are, sprawling by the fire, idling your life away from one meal of gloppy catfood to the next? Or to become a Supercat, seizing your destiny in your claws, and building a better tomorrow for yourself and your fellow felines?

The choice is yours.